DATE DUE			

164735

612.8
WEA

Wearing, Judy.

Taste

Taste

Judy Wearing

Published by Weigl Publishers Inc.
350 5th Avenue, Suite 3304, PMB 6G
New York, NY 10118-0069
Website: www.weigl.com

Library of Congress Cataloging-in-Publication Data available upon request.
Fax 1-866-44-WEIGL for the attention of the Publishing Records department.

ISBN 978-1-60596-056-2 (hard cover)
ISBN 978-1-60596-057-9 (soft cover)

Printed in China
1 2 3 4 5 6 7 8 9 0 13 12 11 10 09

Editor: Heather C. Hudak
Design and Layout: Terry Paulhus

All of the Internet URLs given in the book were valid at the time of publication. However, due to the dynamic nature of the Internet, some addresses may have changed, or sites may have ceased to exist since publication. While the author and publisher regret any inconvenience this may cause readers, no responsibility for any such changes can be accepted by either the author or the publisher.

Every reasonable effort has been made to trace ownership and to obtain permission to reprint copyright material. The publishers would be pleased to have any errors or omissions brought to their attention so that they may be corrected in subsequent printings.

Weigl acknowledges Getty Images as its primary image supplier for this title.

CONTENTS

What is Taste?

How do we know if our food is sweet or sour? Our tongue tells us so. It uses taste to tell us if our food is salty, sweet, sour, bitter, or **umami**. Taste is one of our **senses**. It helps us learn about our surroundings.

Close your eyes, and lick the back of your hand. What do you taste?

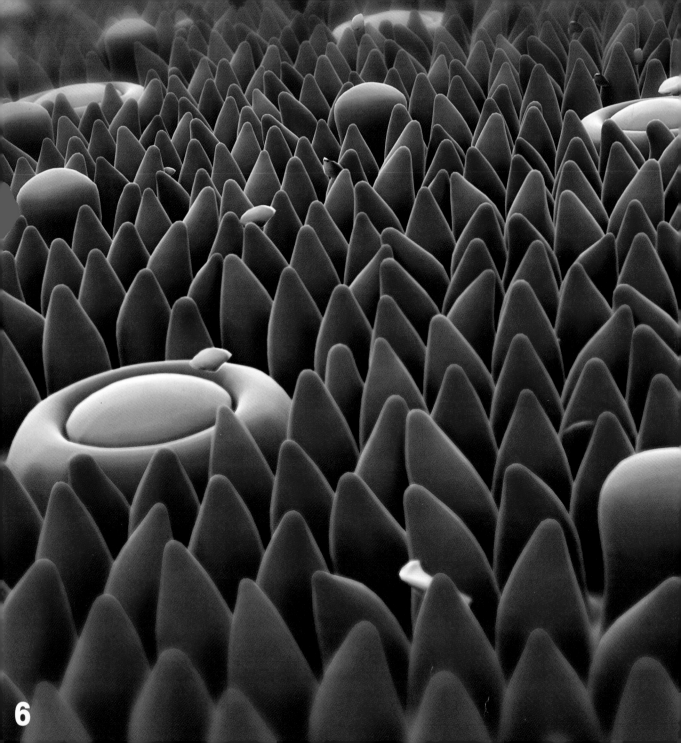

Bumpy Tongue

Can you feel the bumps on the top of your tongue? Each of these bumps has taste buds on it. These tiny buds can detect the **flavor** of anything we put in our mouth.

At birth, people have about 10,000 taste buds. They are too small to see with the naked eye.

Food for Thought

How do taste buds work? Each taste bud has a hole in the top. Liquid from food soaks into the hole. **Cells** inside the hole **detect** the food's flavor. They send this data to your brain. Then, your brain tells you how your food tastes.

Did you know that catfish have taste buds all over their bodies, from the tips of their noses to the ends of their tails?

Super Saliva

What makes you drool? Saliva is liquid that our mouth makes. It breaks down the food we eat and helps it reach the cells in our taste buds. This helps us taste our food.

We can only taste when liquid reaches the taste cells. If there is no liquid, there is no taste.

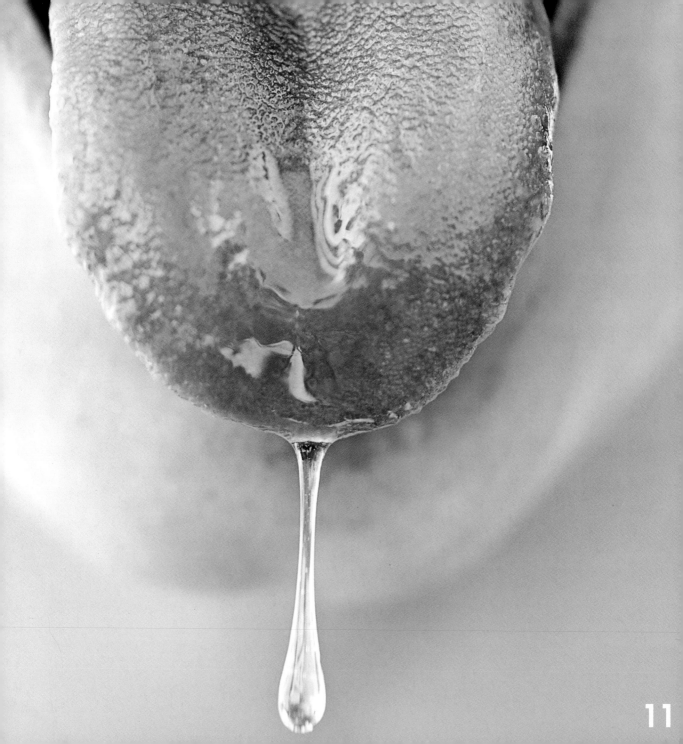

Smart Taste Buds

Do you prefer the taste of honey or cheese? Most people prefer sweet, salty, or umami foods. Often, they are full of **calories.** Our bodies use calories as energy so that we can play sports and do other activities.

Taste can tell us if something is good to eat. Food that tastes sour may be rotten.

After dessert, sweet foods do not taste as sweet.

13

Salty and Sweet

What foods does your body **crave**? This is your body's way of telling you what it needs.

If you have a craving for a salty flavor, your body may need salt. Salt is found in foods such as soup, soy sauce, nut snacks, and crackers.

When your body craves something sweet, it needs sugar. Sugar is found in foods such as fruit, cakes and cookies, candy, and milk.

15

Tongue Twisters

If you suck on a lemon, does your face scrunch up? Lemons are known for their sour flavor. This flavor comes from **acid**.

When you eat bitter food, you may feel like spitting it out. Bitter flavor is found in things such as medicine and coffee.

Different Tastes

How would you describe the taste of broccoli? Ask a friend to describe the taste. Was it the same?

Not everyone tastes things the same way. Green vegetables taste very bitter to some people. Other people cannot taste anything bitter at all.

As people age, they lose taste buds. This is why a child's sense of taste is better than that of an adult. It also explains why some adults like strong-tasting foods, such as spinach and onions.

Taste is Smelly

What happens if you plug your nose while eating? You may not taste your food very well. This is because we use our sense of smell to taste food.

The way the food smells combines with the way it tastes. It is the mixture of taste and smell that makes food taste good or bad.

If you could not smell your food, you would not be able to taste the difference between bananas and pineapples.

Taste Test

Supplies
Paper towel, a partner, a blindfold, a glass of drinking water, small pieces of different dry foods, such as soda crackers, cookies, cheese, and bread

1. Swallow as much of the saliva in your mouth as you can.

2. With the paper towel, dry your tongue well.

3. Have your partner put on your blindfold.

4. Have your partner put a piece of food on your tongue. Can you taste it? What is it?

5. Take a drink of water so that your tongue is wet. Have your partner put the same piece of food on your tongue. Can you taste it now? What is it?

6. Take the blindfold off, and change places. Now, it is your partner's turn. Do all the steps again.

7. What did drying your tongue with a paper towel do to your sense of taste? Can you taste food better when your mouth is wet or dry? Why?

Find Out More

To learn more about taste, visit these websites.

PBS Kids
http://pbskids.org/
dragonflytv/show/
tastetest.html

Kid's Health
http://kidshealth.org/
kid/htbw/tongue.html

Children's University
www.childrensuniversity.
manchester.ac.uk/
interactives/science/
brainandsenses/taste.asp

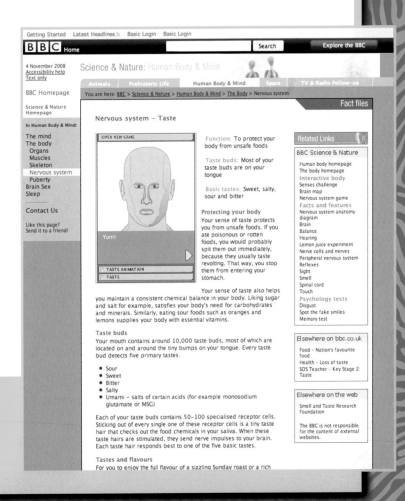

BBC Fact Files
www.bbc.co.uk/science/
humanbody/body/factfiles/
taste/taste_animation.shtml

Glossary

acid: a chemical that tastes sour

calories: units used to measure the amount of energy food produces

cells: the smallest units of the body

crave: a strong desire

detect: to notice something is there

flavor: the way something tastes

senses: the ways the body gets information about what is happening in its surroundings

umami: savory; often found in meat and cheese

Index